The Colonies

The Georgia Colony

Tamara L. Britton

ABDO Publishing Company

visit us at
www.abdopub.com

Published by ABDO Publishing Company, 4940 Viking Drive, Edina, Minnesota 55435.
Copyright © 2001 by Abdo Consulting Group, Inc. International copyrights reserved in all
countries. No part of this book may be reproduced in any form without written permission from
the publisher.

Printed in the United States.

Cover Photo Credit: North Wind Picture Archives
Interior Photo Credits: North Wind Picture Archives (pages 7, 9, 11, 13, 15, 17, 19, 21, 23, 25,
    27, 29)

Contributing Editors: Bob Italia, Kate Furlong, and Christine Fournier
Book Design and Graphics: Neil Klinepier

Library of Congress Cataloging-in-Publication Data

Britton, Tamara L., 1963-
    The Georgia colony / Tamara L. Britton.
        p. cm. -- (The colonies)
    Includes index.
    Summary: Provides a history of Georgia from before the arrival of European explorers
in the sixteenth century to its statehood in 1788.
    ISBN 1-57765-583-4
    1. Georgia--History--Colonial period, ca. 1600-1775--Juvenile literature. [1.
Georgia--History--Colonial period, ca. 1600-1775.] I. Title. II. Series.

F289 .B865 2001
975.8'02--dc21

                                                                    2001022901

Contents

The Georgia Colony

Georgia is a southern state on the Atlantic Ocean. Native Americans first called Georgia home. In about 1540, Europeans began exploring Georgia's land.

In 1730, James Edward Oglethorpe (OH-guhl-thorp) asked King George II for land in Georgia. Oglethorpe wanted to build a colony where poor Englishmen could go to make a fresh start. In 1733, the first English colonists arrived in Georgia.

A board of **trustees** ruled Georgia. Men ran the government and farmed the land. Women worked at home.

In the 1760s, England's **Parliament** began passing new tax laws. The taxes angered the colonists. This led to the **American Revolution**.

The colonists won the war. Then they formed the United States of America. On January 2, 1788, Georgia became the new nation's fourth state.

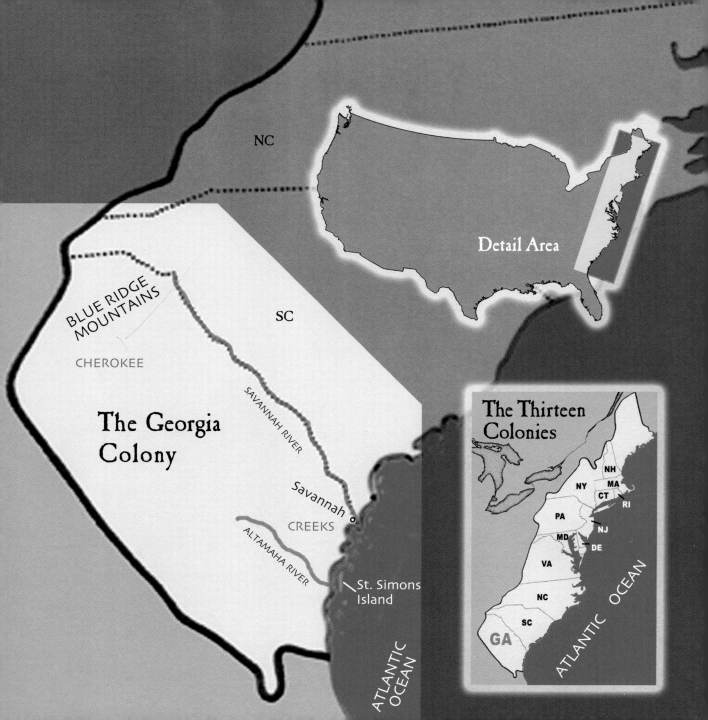

NC

Detail Area

BLUE RIDGE
MOUNTAINS

CHEROKEE

SC

SAVANNAH RIVER

The Georgia
Colony

Savannah

CREEKS

ALTAMAHA RIVER

St. Simons
Island

ATLANTIC
OCEAN

The Thirteen
Colonies

NH

NY   MA

CT

RI

PA

NJ

MD

DE

VA

NC

SC

GA

ATLANTIC OCEAN

Early History

Georgia is on the Atlantic Ocean. The Blue Ridge Mountains are in northeastern Georgia. Central Georgia is a **plateau**. It leads to a low, coastal plain in the south. Many rivers run from the mountains to the ocean.

Native Americans were Georgia's first settlers. Thousands of years ago, people called Mound Builders lived in Georgia. They built huge mounds made of dirt, clay, and rock. Many of these mounds are still standing today.

When the Europeans arrived, Cherokee and Creek tribes dominated the area. The Cherokees and Creeks were excellent farmers. They grew corn, beans, squash, and tobacco.

The Cherokee lived in Georgia's mountains. They had moved there from the north to escape European colonists. The Cherokee spoke Iroquoian (ear-oh-KWOY-an).

The Creeks lived on Georgia's coastal plain. The Creeks were a group made up of many tribes. Many of the Creeks spoke Muskhogean (muhs-KOH-ghee-uhn).

Creeks were governed by chiefs, speakers, officers, and a council.

The First Explorers

The first Europeans to explore present-day Georgia were Spanish. In about 1540, Hernando de Soto led a group of adventurers through the area. They were in search of gold and other riches. But they found nothing.

In 1566, Spaniards traveled to Georgia again. They explored the islands off Georgia's coast. There, they built **missions**. Missionaries converted the Native Americans to Christianity. The Spaniards also built forts on Georgia's islands. The forts protected Spain's claim to the area.

Spain ruled Georgia's coast for more than 100 years. But then French and English colonists began claiming the area. This led to many battles in Georgia.

Slowly, Spain's control over Georgia weakened. By 1721, England had built its first settlement in Georgia. The settlement was called Fort King George. It protected England's colonies from attacks by Spaniards and Native Americans. But the fort was unsuccessful. Colonists abandoned it in 1727.

De Soto and his followers make camp while on their way to Georgia.

Settlement

Englishman James Edward Oglethorpe wanted to start a new colony in America. He hoped to create a place where poor people could start a new life. He also wanted **Protestants** to be welcome there. So Oglethorpe asked King George II for a **charter** in 1730.

Two years later, the king granted a charter to a group of **trustees**, which included Oglethorpe. The charter gave the trustees the land between the Altamaha and Savannah Rivers. The land was named Georgia in honor of the king.

Thousands of people wanted to settle in Georgia. They would receive free passage to America, supplies, and land. So the trustees chose the colonists carefully. Finally, 35 families were selected to make the trip. In November 1732, they left for Georgia on the ship *Ann*.

Oglethorpe and the colonists arrived in February 1733. They settled at present-day Savannah. Creek Chief Tomochichi (toh-MOH-chee-chee) welcomed them. Colonists from the Carolina colonies brought money, animals, tools, and rice.

Oglethorpe meets with Georgia's Native Americans.

Government

The **trustees** ruled the Georgia Colony. They made the colony's laws. But the trustees lived in England. So they sent Oglethorpe to Georgia to represent them. He made sure the colonists followed the trustees' laws.

Oglethorpe organized Savannah into **wards**. Each ward had a community square with lots facing it. A constable governed each ward. Men took turns guarding the wards from attack.

The colony had civil and criminal courts. Judges issued punishments to people guilty of crimes. They put criminals in the **stocks**, dunked them in the river, whipped them, or hanged them. Others had to pay fines or go to jail.

A **militia** (muh-LISH-uh) protected Georgia. In 1742, Spain attacked Georgia's St. Simons Island. Georgia's militia defeated Spain. This conflict is called the Battle of Bloody Marsh. It finally ended Spain's control over Georgia.

In 1752, Georgia became a royal colony. This meant England's king ruled Georgia instead of the trustees. The king named John Reynolds as Georgia's first royal governor.

Reynolds had the power to grant land, command the **militia**, and conduct business with the Native Americans. And he acted as chief judge. A council of 12 men and an assembly also ruled the royal colony.

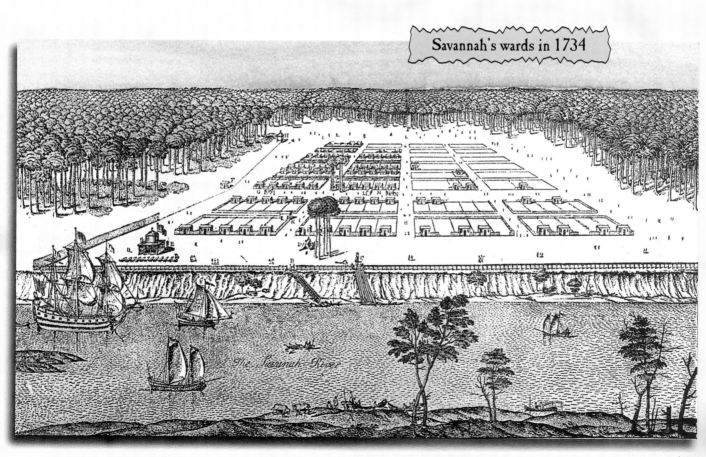

Savannah's wards in 1734

13

Life in the Colony

In the Georgia Colony, men ran the government. And they were responsible for providing food for their families. So they farmed and hunted. Some men also held jobs outside the home as blacksmiths or carpenters.

Women rarely worked outside the home. They raised children and managed the household. Women grew vegetables in the garden, cooked meals, and made clothing. They also preserved food for the winter.

The colonists worked hard. But they had time to celebrate holidays, too. They observed Oglethorpe's birthday and the king's birthday. They ate, drank, and danced to celebrate. The colonists also played cricket and raced horses.

Religion was important to the colonists. Georgia's **charter** forbade Catholics from settling there. But people of other faiths were welcome.

Many colonists belonged to the Church of England. Presbyterians (press-buh-TEER-e-unz) from Scotland and Lutherans from Germany settled in Georgia. Jewish and Moravian colonists also moved there.

Colonists clear a field for spring planting.

Making a Living

Oglethorpe wanted Georgia to be a colony of small farmers. So colonists were limited to 500 acres (202 ha) of land. And slavery was illegal. These measures prevented Georgia's colonists from building huge plantations.

Rice was Georgia's most valuable crop. Farmers grew it along rivers, marshes, and coastal areas. Colonists also grew wheat, corn, peas, and **indigo**. They raised cattle and pigs. **Immigrants** from the Virginia Colony grew tobacco.

The colonists also built sawmills. They made lumber, tar, pitch, and **turpentine**. They traded these products with other countries and colonies.

Though Georgia had some **industry**, it was mostly a farming colony. So, Georgians had to trade rice, pork, and wood products for manufactured goods. Georgians traded with England, the West Indies, and other colonies.

Soon many Georgians wanted to allow slavery. With slaves, they could have bigger farms and make more money. By 1740, the land grants had risen to 2,000 acres

(809 ha) per colonist. In 1749, a new law said Georgia's colonists could have slaves.

By 1778, half of Georgia's population was slaves. Slaves supported Georgia's agricultural **economy** until the Thirteenth **Amendment** was passed in 1865.

Slaves unload rice barges.

Food

Early Georgians had to find their own food. So the men hunted deer, bear, turkey, geese, and ducks. In the ocean and rivers they fished for flounder, shad, and trout. Native Americans taught the colonists how to eat oysters and clams.

Later, Georgians had more food choices. They added to what they hunted and caught with products from their farms. They raised cattle and pigs. They salted and pickled the meat to preserve it for use during the winter months. They grew corn, peas, and squash in their kitchen gardens.

Many of Georgia's first colonists became sick from well water. Many died. Oglethorpe thought the colonists were getting sick from drinking rum.

So the **trustees** made rum illegal. Soon colonists dug a new well. It had good water. But rum was still outlawed. So the colonists drank beer, ale, and wine instead.

Men hunt for ducks in a rice field.

Clothing

Upper-class Georgians wore the fashionable clothing of England. Men wore short pants called breeches. They wore tight-fitting jackets called doublets. Women wore dresses made of linen or silk.

Common families made their own clothes from cotton, wool, or flax. Men grew the cotton and flax and raised sheep for wool. Women spun the cotton, flax, and wool into thread. Then they wove the thread into cloth. From the cloth, they made all of their families' clothing.

Both boys and girls wore dresses until they were eight or nine years old. Then they wore the same styles of clothing their parents wore.

Colonists used roots and berries to dye their clothes bright colors. ⟹

Homes

Georgia's vast pine forests allowed many colonists to build log cabins. The cabins usually had only one room. A large fireplace was on one end of the room. The fireplace's chimney was made of mud and sticks.

Later, the settlers built houses out of **tabby** and bricks. The houses were one story. Most had one room, but some had two rooms. Successful farmers' houses had many buildings to keep living and working areas separate.

In the late colonial period, colonists built two-story houses. These houses had two rooms upstairs and two rooms downstairs. They also had a fireplace and a covered porch.

Wealthy farmers built large houses with many rooms.

23

Children

In the Georgia Colony, many children died when they were very young. Those that survived helped on their parents' farms. The girls helped their mothers with household chores. The boys worked with their fathers in the fields and workshops.

When they had free time, children played with homemade toys. The toys were often made out of wood, corn cobs, or corn husks. Children also played games like hopscotch or cat's cradle.

Some children were able to go to school. Georgia's **trustees** supported elementary education. But there were not many schools. Teaching did not pay much money. So it was hard to find teachers.

In the German settlement of Ebenezer, the Bethesda Orphan House opened. The orphanage became the best school in the colony. In 1768, a school opened in Savannah. But the teachers soon quit because of the low pay. In 1773, the Bethesda school burned down.

A young boy helps his father in the workshop.

Native Americans

Chief Tomochichi was a Creek Native American. He belonged to the Yamacraw (YAW-muh-craw) tribe. Tomochichi was Oglethorpe's friend. In May 1733, Oglethorpe and the Creeks signed a peace treaty. The Creeks and the colonists lived together peacefully.

Colonists traded with Georgia's Native Americans. The colonists offered weapons, gunpowder, and household goods. The Native Americans traded furs for these goods.

Soon, many more colonists arrived in Georgia. The colonists wanted to settle on Native American lands. So the government wanted to move the Native Americans west of the Mississippi River. By 1827, the Creeks had lost all of their Georgia lands.

Georgia's Cherokee lost their lands, too. In 1838, government troops forced the Cherokee to move to Oklahoma. Many people died along the way. Their journey is called the Trail of Tears. Today, many Creeks and Cherokees live on **reservations** in Oklahoma.

Chief Tomochichi

27

The Road to Statehood

By 1763, England had conquered France and Spain for control of North America. But the wars had been costly. The king thought the colonies should help pay the cost.

England's **Parliament** passed the Stamp Act in 1765. It was a tax. It forced colonists to buy stamps for newspapers, playing cards, dice, and legal papers.

Soon, an English stamp master arrived in Georgia. He stamped the required goods. The stamp proved the colonists had paid the tax. Georgia was the only colony to use the stamps. This angered people from other colonies. They thought the stamps were unjust.

In 1767, Parliament passed the Townshend Acts. They taxed glass, china, paint, paper, tea, and other goods. Georgians slowly grew upset with the king. They agreed with the other colonies that the taxes were unfair.

The **American Revolution** began in 1775. The next year, Georgia sent representatives to the **Continental Congress**. They voted to declare independence from England.

In December 1778, England seized Savannah. Colonists finally retook the city four years later. The colonists won the **American Revolution** in 1783. Then they formed the United States of America. On January 2, 1788, Georgia became the fourth state of the new nation.

Today, Georgia is a state with a strong **economy**. It leads the nation in peanut farming and paper production.

Georgia's colonists defend Savannah from English soldiers.

TIMELINE

1540 - Hernando de Soto explores Georgia

1560s - Spaniards build missions and forts along Georgia's coast

1721 - Carolina colonists build Fort King George in Georgia

1727 - Carolina colonists abandon Fort King George

1730 - James Edward Oglethorpe requests a charter for Georgia

1732 - King George II grants the charter for Georgia

1733 - The first colonists arrive in Georgia and found Savannah; the colonists and the Creeks sign a peace treaty

1742 - Battle of Bloody Marsh

1749 - Slavery becomes legal in Georgia

1752 - Georgia becomes a royal colony

1765 - England's Parliament passes the Stamp Act

1767 - England's Parliament passes the Townshend Acts

1775 - American Revolution begins

1776 - Georgia's representatives at the Continental Congress vote for independence

1778 - English troops capture Savannah

1782 - Colonists recapture Savannah

1783 - Colonists win the American Revolution

1788 - Georgia becomes America's fourth state

Glossary

Amendment - a change to the U.S. Constitution.

American Revolution - 1775-1783. A war for independence between England and its North American colonies. The colonists won and created the United States of America.

charter - a written contract that states a colony's boundaries and form of government.

Continental Congress - the body of representatives who spoke and acted on behalf of the 13 colonies.

economy - the way a country uses its money, goods, and natural resources.

immigrant - a person who moves to a new colony or country to live.

indigo - a shrub with leaves that can be used to produce a deep blue dye.

industry - all of a colony's manufacturing plants, businesses, and trade.

militia - a group of citizens trained for war or emergencies.

mission - a church or building used by missionaries. Missionaries are people who spread a church's religion.

Parliament - England's lawmaking group.

plateau - a raised area of flat land.

Protestant - a Christian who does not belong to the Catholic Church.

reservation - land set aside by the government for Native Americans to live on.

stocks - a wooden device with holes to lock a person's head, hands, or feet in place and allow them to be publicly scorned.

tabby - a cement made of lime, sand or gravel, and oyster shells.

trustee - the person in charge of another person's property or affairs.

turpentine - a substance obtained from pine and fir trees.

ward - one of the parts into which a city is divided for the purposes of government.

Web Sites

Georgia History
http://www.cviog.uga.edu/Projects/gainfo/gahist.htm
This site is sponsored by the Carl Vinson Institute of Government at the University of Georgia. It provides links to information on Georgia's native peoples, its exploration, and its colonial history.

This site is subject to change. Go to your favorite search engine and type in Georgia Colony for more sites.

Index